MARTIN D. FINCHAM

# DIARY OF A
# Novice
# NED

A guide to going plural and developing
a portfolio career as a Non-Executive Director

ISBN paperback: 9798589957846

To my wife Joanna,
without whom this work would neither be
possible nor worthwhile.

# CONTENTS

# FOREWORD

When I first heard the expression "I'm going plural" in the 1990s on a call with a CEO who was about to step down, I didn't know what it meant. AltaVista was no help (Google wasn't really a thing yet), so a colleague explained that it was the transition from having one singular executive role to many non-executive board and chair roles. Going plural is rare and little understood for several reasons. Firstly, it requires success typically gained as a CEO that other organisations want to learn from by appointing that individual to their board. Secondly, it requires an individual who, having spent their career running things, is prepared to step back to give advice to others who are running businesses. Finally, it requires a growth mindset to start over again as a novice board member having been a successful CEO. In short, it requires a successful person who is used to calling the shots choosing to be a rookie who is no longer in charge. Sound unlikely? That's why it doesn't happen very often.

When it does happen, people don't often write about it so there aren't many books about "going plural". As Martin specialises in the new world of cloud computing and software as a service (SaaS), books like this are rare and finding one is about as likely as visiting an office in late 2020 (pandemic joke).

Before you go plural, it's really hard to know what the practical implications of a plural career are. This book provides some much sought-after answers. It's full of real and practical tips, such as how much money you might need to invest in the companies you are working with. Yes, you might have to give *them* money. Martin has acted in this way as a business 'angel' investing in companies many times and has a clear perspective on what he looks for. Reading this section is a lot more instructive than watching episodes of *Dragons' Den* or *Shark Tank*. Martin has also led funding rounds from growth capital firms raising many millions of pounds; this book lets the reader into that process.

Many people think of the boardroom as being wood-panelled and filled with grey-haired accountants, driven by governance of agenda items and risk registers. Snore, that's so 20th century. Martin takes us into a completely different world of new economy boardrooms (or Zooms) with some of the fastest-growing companies in the world. The companies that Martin typically works with are scale-ups, growing at least 50% annually and consequently changing all of the time. What works for them one year won't work for the next. Martin's approach to board roles reflects that agility.

Software is becoming an increasingly important part of the world. Martin gives a rare first-hand insight into roles and responsibilities of sitting on the boards of these companies of the future. This book explains in clear words some of the important factors, decision-making and terminology involved. Have you ever wondered what ARR, liquidation preferences, net retention, customer success, making the quarter and share options really mean and why? Wonder no longer.

I have known Martin for many years and am privileged to be one of his ScaleUp Group colleagues. His commitment, passion and enthusiasm for becoming a NED shines through and sets an inspirational example. He has never done things by halves and in my view was a novice board member for about the first three weeks. I thoroughly enjoyed this book and recommend it whether you have gone plural, are thinking about it or are happily singular.

## ADAM HALE
Chairman, ScaleUp Institute and
a member of ScaleUp Group. Adam is, er, plural.

# INTRODUCTION

Why this book and why now? Well, I've long felt that I had the potential to write a half-decent book and I have received sufficient encouragement along my professional journey to keep that suggestion looming large on my personal to-do list. But, as a first-time author, I needed to have my loins well and truly girded by a couple of catalytic events.

Back in December 2019, I was introduced to a business coach and ex-NHS clinical psychologist called John Sutherland. The context was some due diligence work being undertaken by a potential lead investor in a Series B funding round for one of my companies where I am the chairman. They had me meet with John to discuss the dynamics of my relationship with the CEO and wider management team to look at ways to further improve our individual and collective performance. In John's inimitable style, he gave as much as he received – specifically questioning my personal sense of purpose and why I now do what I do (having recently become a pluralist). The short version is that I am motivated to give something back to the industry and country that combined to make upward mobility possible for a young man from a working-class background with no university education. It was John who, with more than a hint of sarcasm, pointed out that, being as I was helping out seven early-stage companies by being on their boards, why not help the next 70 or 700 aspiring entrepreneurs and non-executive directors (NEDs) who could also benefit? In short, my delivery model was not scalable. The obvious answer was to write a book…or two.

The second, and most recent, catalyst was a WhatsApp message that I received just before last Christmas Eve from Simon Hill, founder and CEO of Wazoku. I will tell the full Wazoku story later in this book, as joining their board was my first experience of becoming a non-executive director. Simon wrote, "You want to see something…" which was a tee-up that I gleefully ignored, as no-one likes a show-off. Several minutes later, Simon kindly sent me an Amazon link to the book that he had just co-authored and published with a "Look what Santa did for me!" embellishment. Whilst my first parental-like instinct was to burst with pride, I must confess that only moments later my competitive nature took over and I mischievously thought, "Right mate, I'll take your *One Smart Crowd* tome and raise you *Fincham's First Opus*!"

So here we find ourselves folks. I just hope John was right!

# MY CAREER IN A NUTSHELL

If, like me, you prefer people to establish they are *bona fide* before you start paying much attention to what they have to say, then this chapter is for you. Else please skip ahead now.

I am often asked how I got started so early in the technology industry. Well, in my head, I am the original computer geek. For those old enough to remember, think back to the precocious Milky Bar Kid, but instead of a chocolate pistol I'm waiving a keyboard. As a kid, I was the beneficiary of my father's hobby of tinkering with all things electrical and electronic. This was a skill set that he developed serving on board warships in the British Navy and then transferred into the private sector by working for various military contractors.

By the late 1970s, we were assembling from kits what you would now describe as a personal computer. Back then, a kit meant that you received the parts in a box and needed skills like wire soldering to assemble the electronic components and carpentry to make a wooden box, in which you would mount the keyboard and printed circuit boards. If you were also playing with computers around that time, then your mind is likely now filled with images of cassette tapes (no fancy storage like floppy or hard disks), acoustic telephone couplers for data communications (no modems or internet connections), computer magazines containing code listings for you to key in (no apps to download and install). And when your mum made you turn the computer off at night to save on the electricity bill, then you lost everything and had to start afresh the next morning!

I was lucky to live through the personal computer revolution of the 1980s and develop the technical skills to master this new technology. Along the way, we acquired one of the first Apple Mac 128k machines to arrive in the UK. Overnight I became an evangelist for Apple, and this passion helped me to evolve from a geek into a salesman. I eventually became part of the Apple channel business in the UK, at first selling into the burgeoning desktop publishing market and then eventually specialising in servicing corporate accounts with their sophisticated systems-integration needs. This success launched my sales career and with it a burning entrepreneurial desire.

In 1994, aged 24, I founded my first software company with two ex-colleagues from a systems integrator where, together, we had successfully launched a new line of business. I will tell that fully story if I ever write my autobiography so, for now, let's simply fast-forward to when we sold that middleware business in 2000 – at the height of the Dot Com boom. After this, I moved the family to California and enjoyed an exhilarating few years living in Silicon Valley and attending sales calls, business meetings and a plethora of conferences and other events throughout the United States. As a Brit, these insights were incredibly valuable in helping me to learn how to really do business effectively across all of North America (and not just the east and west coasts). I also learnt how to adjust to the cultural differences as I grew my own team, became part of a US-centric global management team and interacted with many different kinds of customers, business partners and suppliers along the way.

We returned to the UK in 2004 and, having been on a wildly successful ride for the previous ten years, frankly I wasn't sure what I wanted to do next. Initially, I took some time to investigate the state of the angel investing ecosystem in Europe. I was fortunate to have been exposed to the benefits of a well-run angel network when, whilst in Silicon Valley, the late, great Fred Hoar[1] introduced me to the Band of Angels. I had a half-baked idea that I should start a network called the 'Anglo American Angels' through which Silicon Valley investors would be exposed to qualified European deal flow and European starts-up could access smart West Coast angel money. This was a rather novel concept back in 2004.

But what I then found in Europe was, to be honest, a rather ramshackle ecosystem when compared with our sophisticated American cousins, so I shelved the idea and turned my attention to next the ad(venture). On the plus side, I did get introduced to the Cambridge Angels Network during this research project, and they struck me as the only network in Europe that was as well organised as those I had experienced in the Valley. Much later, in 2013, I was fortunate to be invited to join the Cambridge Angels, of which I am still an active member and even did a stint on their board for a few years.

Turning back to my career, I wasn't - for various personal reasons - much in the mood to launch another UK start-up in 2005, and so I got to thinking about developing my professional self in other ways. Having been a Young Turk sales guy, and then a first-time entrepreneur, I figured that I was now kind of unemployable and not likely to ever thrive again just working for 'the man'.

Then, one lazy Sunday morning, I found myself reading the executive appointments section of *The Sunday Times* newspaper. This was not a regular habit, and I didn't subscribe to the paper, so I honestly can't remember why I was doing this…but what turned out to be a fateful opportunity to join an exciting global company leapt off the page.

This was the start of a 12-year journey with one of the most successful software companies ever to come out of the Australasia region; LANSA. Founded some 20 years prior in 1987, LANSA was the brainchild of two serial tech entrepreneurs; one was still actively engaged in the running the business, and the other was a silent partner by the time I joined the company. I foresaw the opportunity to earn my stripes, as well as to gain the trust of the founders, with a view to ultimately taking over the running of this still privately-held business from the founders, who were then into their 60s and thinking about succession or exit.

This opportunity was realised in 2012. After six years of successfully running and growing the EMEA region and then, additionally, the Americas (by then accounting for more than 85%

of all worldwide revenue), I finally took over from the founder and became the new CEO of LANSA. I'm proud to say that, over the following five years, we both scaled and diversified the business, resulting in a seven-fold increase in EBITDA and ultimately leading to an exit to a Private Equity buyer in 2018. It was during these later stages of my time at LANSA that I was offered my first non-executive director role, which influenced the remainder of my career. Towards the end of my tenure, I decided that I would not try to exceed my accomplishments at LANSA by ever pursuing another full-time role. It was time to go plural!

# CURRENT PORTFOLIO

**B**efore launching into the rest of my story, I thought it would be useful to provide a snapshot of my current non-executive roles.

**NED NOTE:**

*"Building a decent portfolio requires a lot of shoe leather. The right roles are not just going to fall into your lap. You have to find them by developing a pipeline of opportunities and raising your profile to eventually turn considerable initial effort into regular inbound interest in hiring you. As you start to reach capacity (say six slots) then you will likely evolve your initial criteria to consider the roundness of your portfolio – for example along diversity lines. A well-constructed portfolio demonstrates that you have the energy and application, which in terms helps to further establish your personal brand."*

## BlackCurve Solutions

**HQ:** London, UK | **My role:** Chairman, joined October 2018

This B2B SaaS company is on a mission to help retailers across the world find 'hidden pockets of profit' in their inventory. The BlackCurve platform is used by eCommerce businesses to make pricing decisions that optimise the profit margin from each product sale. Data science is applied to optimise these pricing recommendations in real-time.

Founded in 2016, BlackCurve was started with a small seed investment, working out of a cottage on the outskirts of London; now, after more than 10,000 days of R&D effort, BlackCurve is making pricing decisions for more than 10m products for eCommerce companies across the world.

In February 2018, the company raised seed funding from Mercia Fund Managers and software entrepreneur and investor, Nick Kingsbury. This investment was used to expand the company's core team across sales, software development and data science. The company closed a £1.5m Seed+ round in April 2019 with new capital from VC Nauta and follow-on participation from Mercia and myself.

At the end of 2020, the company received £1m of new funding in an over-subscribed round. This round was led by me, with participation from Nauta Capital, The Cambridge Angels Network and other prominent angels, and members of the ScaleUp Group. It was then bolstered by a match from the UK Government's Future Fund. The company is on track to hit the metrics that will trigger a Series A round in late 2021.

## SHE Software

**HQ:** Glasgow, Scotland | **My role:** Chairman, joined June 2018

The purpose at SHE Software is to continuously develop a smarter approach to health and safety management in the workplace. Our software helps to improve compliance, boost efficiency and engage workers in a culture of proactive health and safety. I was drawn into their noble mission to make the workplace a safer place for everyone.

The company has been developing health and safety management software for more than 20 years. Founded in Scotland in 1995, more than 300 customers across different business sectors now benefit from using the Assure SaaS platform. The company is truly global, with offices in the UK, US and ANZ.

My friends at the ScaleUp Group helped SHE to secure £3m of Series A funding from NVM Private Equity (now Mercia) in February 2018, and I joined the board shortly thereafter. This initial funding was topped-up by NVM/Mercia before Frog Capital led our £7m Series B round two years later.

SHE is in global scale-up mode and continues to grow rapidly every year. Attitudes toward health and safety in the workplace are, thankfully, improving all of the time. It is no longer practical for companies to quality manage their environment without a fundamental system-of-record for tracking and reporting on their risks, audits and incidents. Directors of UK companies are liable for fines, and potentially jail time, for negligence. Also, in the UK, we are recognised as having some of the best practices for modern health and safety management, which gives SHE a competitive advantage in other markets. There have been frenetic levels of M&A activity in this market, mostly fuelled by private equity, and thus we are regularly approached by potential buyers. The future outlook for SHE Software is very healthy indeed.

## Scoro Software

**HQ**: London, UK | **My role**: Chairman, joined January 2020

Scoro is an award-winning work management software platform for collaborative teams in the professional services and creative industries. Thousands of teams in more than 60 countries trust Scoro to increase their margins, save them time and accelerate data-driven decision-making. Unlike traditional single-use solutions, Scoro is scalable across an entire business – from projects and sales through to billing and reporting.

Impressively, during the Covid-19 pandemic, Scoro joined an elite group of start-ups founded in Estonia that have raised more than $20m in venture capital. Currently, Estonia is the world leader in creating technology unicorns per capita, with successes including Skype, Transferwise, Bolt and Pipedrive.

Work management software became a booming category due to the remote working patterns of creative and professional service businesses. These businesses rushed to stock-up on communication and collaboration tools in 2020, but this influx created new distractions and disruption for teams. Scoro coined the phrase 'Weapons of Mass Distraction' to describe the productivity threat of people constantly switching between SaaS tools, losing focus, duplicating work and risking the loss of data integrity (no single version of the truth).

Since announcing our $16m Series B funding in March 2021, we have a fully-funded business plan to extend our leadership in the SMB market segment as well as continuing to push higher into the enterprise market and entering new territories with native language versions of the product. Perhaps we have another European unicorn in the making?

## Veeqo

**HQ**: Swansea, Wales | **My role**: Chairman, joined March 2020

When I joined Veeqo, after their Series A round (led by Octopus Investments), it was clear that the company was ready to put the region of South Wales on the map. There was more to Veeqo than just being another hot B2B SaaS vendor operating in a buoyant market (in this case, tools for eCommerce). Their founder, Matt Warren, is a man on a mission to help regenerate an economically depressed area – his hometown of Swansea – by creating hundreds of well-paid jobs and hopefully kick-starting the birth of a new tech cluster.

Going on this mission with Matt appealed to me because my wife, Joanna, is from South Wales and so we spend family time there. The region has never recovered from decades of neglect, by successive governments, after losing the vital coal industry and other significant employers like steel manufacturing and the ports. We have teenage nieces still in education there that will soon be out looking for work. Alas such careers are usually built outside of Wales as social mobility is limited when compared to, say, opportunities in England just across the border. It would be good karma for us to have played a small part in creating future job opportunities for our family members and their friends.

Being in the business of selling 'picks and shovels' to the booming e-commerce industry has led to impressive month-on-month growth for Veeqo. Our market segment is also on fire when it comes to M&A activity. Major global software vendors like Intuit, Sage, Descartes and Square have all made acquisitions or investments in this space. Our business plan is to raise a large Series B round in H2 2021 and then accelerate growth past the noteworthy £10m ARR mark and then exit with a valuation of more than £100m. We believe that hitting these milestones would feel significant to both the entrepreneur and investor communities alike, thereby shining a light on Swansea and forever changing perception of the region.

## Essentia Analytics

**HQ**: London/New York City | **My role**: NED, joined March 2020

Essentia is a FinTech business which applies behavioural analytics to improve outcomes for professional investors. Essentia helps both short- and long-term professional investors to mitigate bias, maintain investment discipline and achieve better performance. We articulate these gains as delivering Behavioural Alpha® which, in real terms, has resulted in the median investor generating 150 bps of additional returns over and above their index, per annum.

I was particularly drawn to this opportunity by our impressive founder, Clare Flynn Levy (ex-hedge fund manager and serial tech entrepreneur), and also by the quality of the Essentia board which includes Charles D. Ellis (dubbed "the wisest man on Wall Street" by *Money* magazine) and Kevin Eyres (who started LinkedIn Europe from his spare bedroom in 2007, and ran it to the IPO in 2011). I was introduced to Essentia by my friends at Calculus Capital, who I had enjoyed working with since they led the Series A round at Wazoku in May 2019.

Essentia is on the verge of announcing the details of a substantial investment by a strategic partner, themselves being one of the largest banking institutions in the United States. This investment provides strong endorsement of our vision that, soon, behavioural analytics will become a must-have capability for active fund managers - as essential as having a Bloomberg terminal on their desk. Our new strategic partner increases the reach of our global distribution as they already service several thousand clients that fit our ideal customer profile. Together we will define the *de-facto* standard for the investment community to benchmark themselves against.

## EyeQuant

**HQ**: London, UK | **My role**: NED, joined July 2019

In a world where digital designers are being forced to compete harder for the attention of their users, EyeQuant makes it faster and easier to reach design decisions that increase engagement and conversion. We've christened this technique: data-before-you-launch.

EyeQuant is a predictive AI that delivers instant, objective data on how users will perceive any digital experience, before they see it. EyeQuant is a SaaS business that removes the need for expensive and time-consuming eye-tracking studies by simulating a 200-person study in seconds; streamlining the design process for truly optimised designs. EyeQuant's predictive models analyse more than 1.6m data points across 20,000 experiments involving hundreds of participants to detect which design characteristics evoke human attention within the first three to five seconds. The future of digital design is data-driven and EyeQuant is at the forefront of this emerging field.

I was first introduced to EyeQuant by New Model Venture Capital, where I spent a year as an operating partner providing advice and support across their SaaS portfolio. New Model brought in a new CEO, Charlie Blake-Thomas, to take the business to the next level, and I had the pleasure of working closely with Charlie during those early, formative days. I then left to develop the portfolio that you are reading about here, only to return a year later when Charlie kindly asked me to join their board.

At the timing of writing, EyeQuant had just been accepted into the AI Accelerator at the highly regarded Founders Factory (co-founded by Brent Hoberman). As their chief scientific officer, Jeffrey Ng, said at the time:

> "EyeQuant has an exciting blend of deep neuroscience applied to the art of visual design, for tasks such as creating websites, digital assets, and even

in-store displays. The technology platform shortens the create-deploy-test-iterate cycles of designers by using advanced machine learning and AI models to predict the attention of users and performance of visual assets. We are super excited to work with the team."[2]

Whilst EyeQuant represents one of the smaller companies in my portfolio, they arguably have the largest addressable market as I can readily see a time when every digital designer on the planet has incorporated AI technology like this into their workflow. Virtually every analogue experience is going through a digital transformation right now (accelerated by the pandemic), and therefore EyeQuant's market opportunity is genuinely boundless.

## Wazoku

**HQ**: London, UK | **My role**: Formerly NED, joining August 2016, now Chairman (May 2021)

Ideas are the currency of business and an idea management platform enables organisations to gather, manage, develop, analyse and implement ideas that solve real business problems and identify new opportunities.

Wazoku is a global leader in the idea management software market, a position that was cemented with the acquisition, in 2020, of the assets of US-based open innovation firm InnoCentive. In doing so, we created the world's most comprehensive and powerful innovation platform and community. Following a brief partnership earlier in 2020, it became clear that the combination of platform and network had huge value to innovation-focused businesses and was a unique proposition in the market. This transaction was the first significant acquisition by one of my portfolio companies and became an interesting learning experience from a NED perspective (as an operator I had bought and sold several companies before).

Wazoku now provides the world's biggest innovation community and broadest innovation offering. It allows the crowdsourcing of solutions to any pressing business challenge, all supported by the features and functionality found in the Wazoku SaaS platform, Idea Spotlight, which has enjoyed more than ten years of development and customer-led product evolution. I talk more about Wazoku in the 'Landing your first NED role' chapter, as this was my first role.

# PROFESSIONALISING MY HOBBY

W hy have I chosen this seemingly odd title for my chapter about preparing yourself for a plural career? Well, firstly, this phrase accurately describes what I actually did; I took a series of activities that were just personal hobbies, side hustles, altruistic endeavours, passion projects etc. and gave them a professional upgrade. Secondly, now that I have the benefit of hindsight, I would advocate approaching the transition in this way. One of the benefits of being a pluralist is that you are free to juggle multiple roles, so why not learn the ropes alongside doing your day job? I see little upside in just diving straight in, albeit I can see how a more sudden switch could be made by, say, an entrepreneur who exited rather abruptly. But, even in this case, I would still advise taking it slow and just listening and learning for the first year or so.

My framework for getting started (with your preparations) has six pillars, each of which requires some practice in order to master the art of being a successful pluralist:

1. Learn about angel investing.
2. Find some entrepreneurs to mentor.
3. Evolve your emotional intelligence.
4. Put aside the cash you are going to need.
5. Develop your personal brand.
6. Build-out your professional network.

Before digging into the 'why' and 'how to' for each pillar, I will stress that I give each one equal weighting in terms of their importance. All six are required in the end product, but the sequencing is less important. It is most likely that you will develop each art in parallel, being somewhat opportunistic about which you practice and when, and the speed of progress along each one.

## ANGEL INVESTING

You might be asking yourself: what has learning how to be a successful angel investor got to do with becoming an effective non-executive director (NED)? I will answer that question in a couple of different ways.

Firstly, knowing what a good business opportunity looks like is an intuitive skill that is best honed by reviewing as many such opportunities as possible. I've found that being on the receiving end of hundreds of pitches (for funding) is the fastest way to achieve total immersion. Like developing your golf or tennis swing, you can't learn by simply reading a manual or watching a few YouTube videos. There is no substitute for whacking a few thousand balls. Besides, entrepreneurs are always looking for new money, so those meetings are the easiest to arrange.

Being part of an angel network is even better, as the group will you to sort the wheat from the chaff, organise pitching events and you will benefit from watching more experienced angels do their thing. These fellow angels will become an important part of your network and a source of more than just joint deals; I've learned many things from experts in adjacent fields as well as finding participants for my own fundraising rounds, making some good friends along the way and even sourcing my first NED role.

Note that to become an angel investor in the UK, and likely other jurisdictions, you must first qualify as a 'high net worth individual' or 'sophisticated investor' under specific criteria laid down by the local regulator. In the case of the UK's Financial Conduct Authority, the criteria, at time of writing, was as follows:

> If you earn at least £100,000 a year or have net assets excluding property and pensions of at least £250,000, you can self-certify yourself as a high net worth individual (HNWI)

To qualify as a sophisticated investor, you must:

- have made at least one investment in an unlisted security in the previous two years; or
- have been a member of a business angel network for at least six months; or
- have worked in a professional capacity in the provision of

finance to SMEs in the last two years or in the provision of private equity; or

- be, or have been within the last two years, a director of a company with a turnover of at least £1m.

Please check the current rules on the FCA or your local regulator's website. These rules are in place to protect 'joe public' from being exploited by exposure to investments where they are not well-equipped to judge the risks and/or to put capital at risk which they can ill afford to lose. Promoters of such investments (like start-ups raising money) need to have a 'reasonable belief' that you have self-certified. The self-certification must be in writing, but a promoter can accept verbal assurance that someone has self-certified as a sophisticated investor or HNWI. Once someone has been accepted, the protections are removed for investors in regard to the promotion of securities by someone authorised under the Financial Services Act. Appropriate 'risk warnings' must, however, still be included in all promotional material; these warnings are often absent when founders pitch their start-ups (to investors) so please adopt a *caveat emptor* approach.

If you do make an angel investment deal (in the UK) then you are likely to be exposed to one, or both, of the tax relief investment schemes that the Government offers to encourage investment in small businesses. These are the Seed Enterprise Investment Scheme (SEIS) and Enterprise Investment Scheme (EIS). A full discussion about these schemes is beyond the scope of this chapter, but I will return to them later in the book when we talk about the potential upside (financial income and investment returns) from the portfolio that you will build.

I said that I would also answer the 'why become an angel investor' question another way: in my opinion, there is no quicker way to learn how professional investors think and act than to shadow them as an angel. Many things magically crystallise in your mind when your own money is at risk! But why do we even need to get inside the minds of professional investors? Because, as a NED, you will inevitably be working with them on your boards and you will also be asked to scrutinise various funding decisions during the life of the company.

Additionally, as a chairperson, you will be expected to lead funding rounds (likely from Series A onwards), and I found that turning from the 'poacher' to the 'game-keeper' was helpful in building rapport and establishing my credentials. For instance, I've never pitched a deal to a fund that I haven't already invested in personally myself or where I intend to come in alongside on the same terms. The investment-making decision that experienced angels and their networks make, along with the resulting due diligence processes they follow, are invariably lighter in nature than, say, how a venture capital firm would act; but the similarities are close enough to make you a contributor rather than a laggard.

## MENTORING ENTREPRENEURS

Providing support and advice to founders and their teams is, for me, the most rewarding part of being on a board. I tend to engage with them on a regular basis and certainly more frequently than the monthly/quarterly cycle of board meetings. In my opinion, if you aren't excited about developing these mentor/mentee relationships, then I wouldn't even bother heading in the plural direction. I suppose one could say that you need to feel the same kind of satisfaction that teachers and parents feel when they help children grow and develop, hopefully at an accelerated rate.

If there is one thing that a good entrepreneur will hustle for even more than funding, then it is receiving free advice and useful intros. They might even offer to buy you the coffee, but they will certainly give you 30 minutes of their time if they see value in the exchange. My point is that it should not be difficult to immerse yourself in their world if you have knowledge, expertise, experience and/or connections that are tangible and obvious. In terms of where to start, the answer is simply to start hanging out where they congregate, for example:

- Events, especially those held in local tech clusters like Cambridge or Shoreditch.
- Pitching sessions, often organised by angel networks, incubators/accelerators, venture firms, university offices (spinouts), business schools and so forth.
- Online, whether that be reading about them in the start-up media and reaching out, finding them on LinkedIn, participating in topic-specific meet-ups etc.

Once again, practice makes perfect, and I found that the years of pro-bono mentoring that I did as a hobby stood me in good stead once I professionalised my activities. You will find that there is a greater diversity of person and thought in entrepreneurial land, and it can take some time to adjust to their mannerisms and learn which relationships are for you and how to optimise your style of engagement for each. This experience will prove invaluable as you decide which boards to join, as the chemistry between you and the founder(s) is a critical success factor and one that I will expand upon further in the next chapter.

## EVOLVING YOUR EMOTIONAL INTELLIGENCE (EQ)

If I was ever going to fail in my transition to going plural, then it would have been here! I've known since a school entry test that my IQ is higher than average. I've found most things easy to learn along the way (except, alas, foreign languages) and invariably held my own when amongst smart people. But it's fair to say that I've had more than my fair share of EQ-related incidents during my career! I can still vividly remember the first time I became aware of my limitations.

This series of incidents came about after an acquisition where I found myself part of an increasingly dysfunctional senior leadership team. When business performance was good, the team worked well together. But when a recession hit, the teamwork and collegiate atmosphere disintegrated overnight.

This dynamic was exacerbated by remote working, with a growing amount of 'them' (field) versus 'us' (HQ) friction. All classic management guru stuff. So classic, in fact, that the brilliant business author Patrick Lencioni had captured our company perfectly in his first leadership fable, *The Five Dysfunctions of a Team*. There was even a protagonist called Martin!

According to the book, the five dysfunctions are:

- Absence of trust – unwilling to be vulnerable within the group.
- Fear of conflict – seeking artificial harmony over constructive passionate debate.
- Lack of commitment – feigning buy-in for group decisions creates ambiguity throughout the organisation.
- Avoidance of accountability – ducking the responsibility to call peers on counterproductive behaviour which sets low standards.
- Inattention to results – focusing on personal success, status and ego before team success.

Working our way through resolving each of these dysfunctions was a painful, yet emotionally enlightening, experience for me. During those few months, I learned more about myself, and my interactions with others, than at any other time in my life.

I even took my first Myers-Briggs® personality test (I have a Commander ENTJ profile[3]). Rather than dismiss these insights as mumbo-jumbo – which is how my younger self might have responded – instead I figured out how to mirror and match different personality types to adapt my style to best work with other people. Had I never gone through this tough patch, I'd likely still be part of the problem rather than part of the solution each time there is conflict in a relationship and/or team.

Why do I consider that balancing your EQ with your IQ is such an essential skill to develop as a pluralist? The answer is that you will likely be transitioning from an executive (wielding power) to a non-executive (having influence), and this change can be challenging for those with a dominant personality. Adjusting to this change was something that I focused on a lot during my first year on the board of Wazoku. I would liken the principle to that of practising *active listening* or, in my case, practising *active not-talking*!

I found that being more aware rapidly improved my note-taking skills, and I developed the patience, and good manners, to ask my questions at the most appropriate juncture rather than interrupting or hijacking the conversation in mid-flow. Upon reflection, I was more dominant in the room during my CEO days and now I feel that I am a much better all-round team player – albeit still guilty of the occasional rant and rave!

## SETTING ASIDE THE CASH YOU ARE GOING TO NEED

Hold on! A career that is going to cost you money? What gives? You thought this was a way to make a living and now you have to invest? Well, yes and no.

I will discuss getting paid in a later chapter but, in terms of preparing for the change, I recommend that you do two things.

Firstly, wait until you have a 'rainy-day fund' that is equivalent to two years of net salary based upon your recent earnings history. Of course, if you don't need all of that bonus money to live well then you can reduce your target accordingly. My point is that, whilst you can earn annual fees as a NED, in my experience this will not become a decent annual salary until you hold four to six roles. That size of portfolio can easily take two years to build, and possibly longer. So, unless you are already financially independent, you must set aside a buffer.

Secondly, expect to make a financial investment in every company that you join. This kind of skin-in-the-game is expected about half of the time in my experience; particularly when professional investors are involved. Besides, if an opportunity is worth your time then surely it is worth some of your money as well?

The potential upside from the investment can be greater than the sum of the annual fees – especially when you contrast rates of income tax with capital gains tax and reliefs like EIS – and therefore investing is the smart thing to do financially if you can afford it. A half-way house would be to apply deferred fees (say six months) to purchase equity in lieu of an actual cash transaction, although this approach would not qualify for any special schemes like EIS. As a chairman, you would always be expected to invest, so think about the size of your pot and the number and type of roles you can realistically afford to undertake. Personally, I budget for making an investment of £25,000 to £50,000 per company, which means that a six-company portfolio could require having a £300,000 pot available for investment.

If you apply rough maths to everything that I've said above, including having an income buffer, then the going plural budget total could be in the order of £500,000. I am not trying to scare you off with this headline number; in fact, quite the opposite. But I do feel that it is important to highlight this stuff before you dive in. Of course, as it takes several years to build such a large portfolio, you don't need to have all of the money in your bank account on day one. I've also seen portfolios built for less, especially where the focus has been on seed stage companies (say less than £1m ARR in SaaS) where the requirements, and quantum, for investments are lower and the use of deferred fees is more commonplace. Having said all of that, I couldn't imagine getting started, and then succeeding, for less than £100,000 – about the total cost of studying an MBA at a top school, so you can decide which route is best for you!

## DEVELOPING YOUR PERSONAL BRAND

The fact that I have written a book about going plural means that the concept is not new. Please know that there are thousands of people out there already doing this work and assume that there are thousands more waiting in the wings. So, what is going to be your identity and professional reputation? How are you going to be found in a keyword search? Why is a board going to choose you from a shortlist of six candidates? It is true that hiring for board members still involves some consideration of image and prestige as well as substance; although I like to think much less so in private early-stage business than public boards appointments where high-profile industry figures and city grandees are in demand. Your accomplishments and references will always speak the loudest, but it's never too soon to figure out your personal brand and then to start marketing yourself accordingly.

For me the positioning was obvious – I am Mr. B2B SaaS. I was already writing and speaking on this topic and, with a 30-year career in the enterprise software business behind me, my background was substantive. But I also faced a quandary: did I want to be pigeon-holed in B2B SaaS or did I want to explore my new-found freedom as a pluralist to diversify into other sectors? I kept an open mind on this dilemma by deciding in advance that at least 50% of my portfolio would be in B2B SaaS (so three roles) and then, down the line, I would re-evaluate how to fill the remaining slots. Needless to say, as a rolling stone likes to gather no moss, momentum became such that I filled my entire portfolio with 100% B2B SaaS companies in what I now consider to be 'cohort #1'. So, I will save the potential exploration of new sectors for my second cohort in the years ahead.

Exploring the various techniques for building your brand are beyond the scope of this section but think of the process as a long-running marketing campaign and don't be reticent to seek help – and even pay for experts if you need them. I suggest that the first step is updating and optimising your LinkedIn profile. A professional brand expert will polish your profile for c. £1,000.

## BUILDING-OUT YOUR PROFESSIONAL NETWORK

As an early adopter of LinkedIn – being member #137,125 from January 2004 – it's safe to say that I've always taken my professional networking seriously. However, even with a prolific global network of contacts developed over decades, I still found that I needed many new connections to first assist with, and then to accelerate, my transition into pluralism. Two categories mattered the most to me.

The first was finding existing pluralists. Back in 2017, when I first got serious about making the change, I found this whole prospect of going plural, and building a portfolio of non-executive roles, to be a dark art. The concept was simple, but the implementation details were scarce – hence why I've now written this guide. It was fortuitous that in 2015 I was invited to a special kind of tech conference called 'Snowball'. I say 'conference', but the event is like no other. In the words of the event organiser:

> "Conferences...everyone's been to those. Off keynotes, 'notworking', shabby hotels, cardboard food and watery coffee. Snowball is different. Over the years, Snowball has curated extraordinary experiences, designed to delight. Successful businesspeople don't always find the time to build enduring relationships, so Snowball facilitates transformative introductions that often prove life changing. Time away from work, family and pressure opens the mind. The catalytic discussions provoke fresh thinking. Imagine all this, blended with a snowy backdrop of winter sports and 5-star luxury accommodation."

If you are excited by this proposition, as was I, then please be aware that this is an invitation-only event. You need to be sponsored, like when joining a private members' club. My advice is to check out www.snowball.net and see if you happen to be connected to any members of their 'Snow Board' (pun intended).

By attending this event for a few years – actually five in a row – I met more than 100 new and interesting people; a handful of which were pluralists who graciously gave me their advice and made other relevant introductions. I will thank each by name in the 'Acknowledgements' section. So that's one category of new network building that I've covered: fellow pluralists.

The second category is professional investors: serious business angels, venture capitalists and private equity. For me, not having had to raise money for more than 20 years, this meant virtually starting from scratch. My angel network was already pretty good, by virtue of my membership of Cambridge Angels and their affiliates. Some professional investors were also part of this Cambridge ecosystem and I had some Snowball alumni members on my list – so I had a couple of places to get started.

I've since found that the better investment firms are always interested in hearing from potential NEDs, so just get busy connecting with them in the usual ways. Some houses (like BGF and Mercia) maintain internal databases and have dedicated resources to growing and developing their own NED networks, like running events for current and future NEDs.

In case it isn't obvious, the reason that these investor relationships are so important is that the investor is often either the trigger for the new hire – for example bringing in an independent chairman alongside their Series A/B round – or they have great influence on who gets hired. Best of all, each investor has their own large and growing portfolio, which means multiple future opportunities for you if you get known by them and do a good job.

# LANDING YOUR FIRST NED ROLE

The path that you choose to take is determined mainly by whether you are seeking only paid roles or those where you can do some good. I've often heard it said that the easiest way to gain some board experience is to start with the non-profit sector, where the barriers to entry are presumed to be lower. This anecdote may well be true, but I chose to pursue only paid (or at least compensated) roles in the beginning.

Why? Because, after a lifetime in the sales profession, I knew that the perceived value of 'free' is close to zero in the mind of the buyer. I did not want to start benchmarking the value of my work at this level. Whilst I wasn't expecting to play in the premier league from day one, I was willing to compete for paid roles against more experienced pluralists.

Arguably, there is a juxtaposition to be balanced when you first enter the market. On one hand, you will benefit from having a certain kind of professional profile. For me, this was being a recently-exited CEO of a mid-size global software company (250-plus employees servicing 7,000-plus customers in 60-plus countries) as well as having been an entrepreneur earlier in my career. This experience demonstrated that I could relate to founders – actually, more importantly, that they could relate to me as they typically don't click with corporate types – and also that I had the scale-up expertise that investors crave. I suppose that my time in Silicon Valley added some additional sparkle. But, on the other hand, as you navigate the transition, I think it is essential to be modest in setting your expectations and humble in your demeanour. I say this because, whilst your accomplishments thus far are part of what makes you attractive as an adviser, you have yet to prove yourself around the boardroom table.

### NED NOTE:

*"If you've achieved a reasonable amount of success, such that people are actually interested to listen to what you have to say and pay you for it, that's the ticket to the game. But you're only as good as your last exit. That's a healthy mindset – I've seen people stumble where they've maybe swaggered a little bit too much."*

In the NED/chair world, you are only as good as your last scale-up success story and this is usually measured by lucrative exits for the investors. So, until you have some *scores on the doors*, I feel that modesty is the best policy. I still feel this way today, three years into my journey, as whilst my portfolio has hit some significant milestones during my tenure, we have yet to record a spectacular exit. This is not unusual as you can expect the average time-to-exit to be three to five years from when you first join the board of a company. It is rare, especially in the UK, to experience exits in less than three years because the predominance of EIS/VCT structures means that investors are disincentivised from exiting any sooner else they lose their tax relief.

In the previous chapter, I covered the preparation stages, which included developing your personal brand, sowing the seeds (for growing new opportunities) by expanding your network and finding some mentors to guide and assist you. By now you are probably asking: so how did Martin find his first NED role? Well, in a classic example of "do as I say, not as I do", I must confess that lady luck handed me that opportunity…and at first, I said no thank you to the offer.

This is the story of Wazoku. I first met its founder, Simon Hill, at a Cambridge Angels (CA) pitching event in late 2014. I remember giving Simon a particularly hard time with my questions, as I was the resident software/SaaS expert in the room and thought I should battle test their value proposition and go-to-market plan. Also present was John Yeomans, who had led the first round of CA investors a year earlier and subsequently joined the board of Wazoku as chairman. Six months later, John invited me to meet with Simon again and soon thereafter the notion of my joining the board was floated. I was very busy running LANSA at the time and, whilst the idea of pursuing a plural career thereafter was in the back of my mind, I was not inclined to act upon it. I held them at arm's-length for another year before Simon made me an offer that I could not refuse. In all seriousness, I owe both John and

Simon a debt of gratitude as, without their doggedness, I may never have started down this path...let alone be writing a book about my experience. Furthermore, John became one of those mentors I've spoken about. I joined the board of Wazoku in August 2015, which means that we are approaching our five-year anniversary at the time of writing and it has been both an incredible ride and a learning experience. In Simon's own words:

> *"We spent 18 months searching for the right commercially-experienced NED. Martin was our unanimous #1 choice. Joining an existing board as the business was scaling-up, he has provided invaluable insight, practical advice and a tough but balanced approach to help guide the business."*

Over those few years, we have more than tripled the Annual Recurring Revenue (ARR) of Wazoku, hired 50-plus people, won global customers and household names, enhanced our investor base from angels to institutional funding (Calculus Capital has thus far invested £3.5m) and completed one acquisition that rewrites the rules of the game in the innovation and idea management space. Not bad for a first gig! Suffice to say that I am very proud of all that the team has achieved and I'm looking forward to helping them to navigate their next big growth spurt and eventually to exit, most likely to a strategic acquirer.

Whilst re-telling this story, I was reminded of the time when Simon and I sat down to discuss the terms of our deal. I had no idea what a compensation package might look like for such a role, but I wasn't motivated by the money as I already had a well-paid job. I figured there would be an equity component (stock options) but, knowing that the company was angel-funded at that point, I didn't necessarily expect to see any monthly fees coming my way.

I said to Simon: "The answer is yes [I accept your offer] regardless of the package, but if you are currently paying board fees to anyone then I'll have what they are having, assuming that my level of effort will be commensurate with theirs." Well, it turns out that paying board fees for top talent, even for an early-stage business, is quite customary; not least because some investors charge annual board monitoring fees to cover their investment director seat, and so this precedent sets the bar for the rest of us.

I know that this [paying of board fees] is a sensitive topic with angel investors, and some venture capitalists (VCs), who feel that every penny raised should be channelled into growth capital and not siphoned out of the side door in board fees. As an angel investor myself, I can empathise with this point of view; although, providing that the fee levels are reasonable, I believe that the tangible value of having an expert, well-engaged board member on your team can return their fee many times over.

For instance, there are numerous times when I have saved my portfolio companies the equivalent of my annual fee in my first few months on the job, usually by stopping money being wasted on activities that I know don't work. At the other end of spectrum, I have led investment rounds of up to £10m without the company needing to engage an intermediary adviser/broker. They would typically charge 5% of the amount raised, plus require a small monthly retainer for the duration – so that's £500,000 plus savings, which would cover 10 years of a chairman's typical annual fee.

### NED NOTE:

*"A mundane but essential safeguard is to protect yourself with Directors & Officers Liability Insurance. This is liability insurance payable to the directors and officers of a company, or to the organisation itself, as indemnification for losses or advancement of defence costs in the event an insured suffers such a loss as a result of a legal action brought for alleged wrongful acts in their capacity as directors and officers. Most companies will already have such an insurance policy in place, but a fledging start-up may not. I choose to maintain my own annual cover (with Hiscox) for peace of mind.*

# FROM NED TO CHAIR

B efore I launch into telling the story of how I came to be offered my first chair role, with the first gig always being the hardest to find, I do not recommend actually starting your journey here. Instead, I advise that you test yourself in a regular NED role first, ideally for a couple of years, before you entertain stepping up to chair a board. I think it's unlikely that you would be offered the chance to jump straight in at the deep-end anyhow; and I would question the motivation, and the qualifications, of any party making such an offer. Of course, there are always outliers, but I learned so much from watching an experienced chairman at work[4] that I simply can't imagine how anyone could do a proper job without this kind of exposure.

### NED NOTE:

*"The tasks and responsibilities of the chair role can run to several pages in a letter of appointment. But simply know this: you are expected to be the bridge between management and shareholders (investors). That may*

*sound like a straightforward place to exist - I promise
you that it is not always comfortable!*

So, to the SHE Software story. I was introduced to their CEO,
Matthew Elson, by my good friends at the ScaleUp Group. I
became a member of this illustrious group of founders and industry
executives shortly after going plural. Started by UK software
industry legend John O'Connell – who founded Staffware, which
sold to TIBCO for $200m back when that was considered a large
exit in the UK – the ScaleUp Group (SUG) provides advisory
services to early-stage technology companies as they approach their
scale-up moment. This is usually once a start-up has passed £1m+
ARR and is considering raising their first significant institutional
investment round (Series A). In John's own words:

> *"We created ScaleUp to help take successful technol-
> ogy start-ups to an even higher level of achievement
> in terms of capability and international growth. We
> achieve this through a unique combination of support,
> advice and finance provided by serial entrepreneurs
> who have been on similar journeys."*

In 2018, SHE Software was an early beneficiary of the ScaleUp
process, receiving £3m in funding from NVM Private Equity as
result of the multiple offers that the SUG network secured for them.
That was around the same time that I joined SUG. When SHE
started looking for a chairman after closing their Series A, they

spoke with several SUG members, and other external candidates, and eventually chose me.

I was particularly drawn to the opportunity of working with Matthew, as the transformation of the business under his recent ownership was impressive (he had acquired SHE in a distressed state from the previous owners for the nominal £1). The company had consistently recorded growth rates of more than 60% and, having secured a market-leading position in the UK, seemed well positioned for global expansion in a huge market with a must-have product. I also felt that I would learn from working alongside NVM's investment director, Charlie Winward, who has a great track record as a tech investor and who struck me as more operationally savvy than your average finance type. This kind of tight board, without excessive representation, was the ideal place to cut my teeth, and I must say that the chemistry has worked well.

### NED NOTE:

*"My best days as a chair are when I know I helped one plus one equal three. Where we sat down to figure something out, and we found the answer. And I know in my heart, I never would have got there by myself, and neither would they. Those moments are golden."*

We have been able to both protect and enhance this positive board dynamic as the company continued its meteoric rise. The board has evolved with two new additions: renowned tech investor, Mike Reid, of Frog Capital, who led our £7m Series B round; and

Jason Warren, who ensured continuity when he stepped up from his previous role of board observer to replace Charlie, who moved on from NVM after they were acquired by Mercia Asset Management.

What lessons can be drawn from my time at SHE that might be helpful to you? Firstly, this was a good example of the power of networking. Had I not been a member of the ScaleUp Group then I doubt that SHE would have found me and, as they ran the search process themselves rather than using a recruiter, I doubt that I would have found them. Whilst I was well known as a B2B SaaS expert, I had no prior exposure to the health and safety software market and, as SHE is headquartered in Glasgow, I wouldn't have stumbled across them whilst running around my home patch in London. This was a classic example of an unadvertised job opportunity.

I do believe that practising your art with a small, simple board structure is the ideal place for a novice to start. For example, I have since chaired a board with three first-time co-founders which, frankly, could be a handful at times. Likewise, I currently chair a board with three investor directors, which can take disproportionately more effort to marshal than with one. These are all skills that you will readily develop over time – like learning to parent one child vs. handling triplets – but you wouldn't choose to start with the triplets. Not wishing to sound patronising, but you will also find that the maturity of your early board members will heavily influence your experience. It is just easier to sail through stormy waters with level-headed co-pilots who have seen it all before and have the T-shirt to show for it. Not only are they less likely to be phased when problems arise, thereby avoiding displays of histrionic behaviour, but they usually know what to do so you also learn from them at an accelerated rate. Sitting at the intersection of so much cumulative wisdom, garnered from a portfolio of boards, is a rare and privileged place to be. You will soon find that learning how they solve problems, and adopt best practice, makes you an even more valuable contributor, and this virtuous cycle spins faster each day.

# IS THERE SUCH A THING AS TOO SMALL?

A primary driver for doing what I now do is altruism; my wish to give back to the industry that has served me so well. Having worked internationally for my whole career (I remember travelling with Apple to Boston, USA, for Macworld Expo aged just 21), I am now passionate about helping to unleash the potential of our UK and European tech ecosystems which have long sat in the shadow cast by our North American cousins. Our collective engineering prowess on this side of the pond is second to none, but it's fair to say that our commercialisation and scale-up expertise can be a step or two behind our global competitors. With my functional skills being in sales and marketing and having global operating experience in the Americas and Asia Pacific, I feel that I should be doing my bit here in Europe to level the playing field.

As a passive angel investor, I am used to dealing with companies at their seed stage, so there is no such thing as *too small of a company* for me to get involved with as an investor. But, when it came to being actively involved in growing a business, I found myself wondering where the line should be drawn? Obviously a two-person business coming out of an accelerator with little more substance than a slide deck and a minimum viable product (MVP) is not likely to be prioritising how to build their first board of directors. But they might need a figure head (let's use the title of chairman) to bring proven business acumen, growth management and fundraising skills that the first-time founders haven't yet acquired. This scenario is most likely if both founders are of a technical nature.

As I considered the eventual size and shape of my portfolio, I decided that I would be open to exploring a few very small businesses. For instance, with a portfolio size of seven, one could choose to have two seed stage, two start-up and two scale-up companies with a non-profit organisation thrown in for good measure. However, this decision was arguably a mistake. It turns out that there *is* such a thing as too small…and it's when you use a sledgehammer to crack a nut. I do not regret the experience though.

One of the many benefits of going plural is that you can operate in multiple segments of the technology industry at the same time. This freedom is especially liberating when break-through technologies start to gain market traction and you find that you can participate in the commercialisation of multiple cool technologies in parallel; examples being Artificial Intelligence, Blockchain and Immersive (VR/AR). When a VC I was working with introduced me to an immersive technology business in Brighton, I was immediately captivated by their value proposition and the strength of the founding team.

Gorilla in the Room is an immersive research technology

company. They are pioneering the application of AR and VR in market research. Their product innovation platform is used to accelerate new product development and point-of-sale strategy. From initial product concepts to shopper marketing, their platform transforms images on 2D screens into real 3D consumer experiences. Real-time data on consumer behaviour accurately predicts the products people love and the retail solutions which drive sales.

I felt that the founding team of three had the perfect blend of expertise to genuinely disrupt a multi-billion-dollar global market that, despite selling insight services to their customers, had not innovated far beyond applying basic market research tools like surveys, pack tests, shopper diaries, in-person focus groups and the like. I joined the company as chairman and we set about productising what had been a services-led, project-based business. It was felt that a SaaS model would allow the company to scale in the most capital-efficient way, but the journey to a true self-service model would take several years to complete.

The company ran very lean and had delivered an MVP of a sophisticated, mobile VR/AR within the limitations of the modest amount of seed capital provided by Mercia Asset Management. My first job as chairman was to raise additional capital to fund the commercialisation phase of the company's development. I succeeded by leading a round with the Cambridge Angels.

With the financial runway secured, we set about formulating and executing the detailed business plan for growing revenue (at least doubling in size every year) and developing the product roadmap. Whilst I enjoyed my time collaborating with the team, and together we made good progress during our first year, I must confess that I grew frustrated at times. On reflection, I put this frustration down to two elements: a minor clash of mindsets (services vs. product) and the relatively slow pace of progress that a lean team could reasonably be expected to achieve within highly-constrained resources.

I was simply used to having more resources to execute in parallel; it was like a mismatch of gears where the drive shaft is trying to make the wheels spin too fast and…crunch…things break and the engine falters. One solution would have been to 'fix the fault' and restart the engine. But, after deliberating hard and thinking broadly about compatibility across my portfolio, I decided that the mismatch was too great and that both parties would be best served by parting ways and finding more compatible partners.

For the record, I am still a huge supporter of the business and do expect it to fulfil its potential (not least because I am its largest angel investor). Earlier I characterised this mistake as using a sledgehammer to crack a nut, and this is the learning that I, and you, can take away from this cautionary tale. Investing in an early-stage company, and joining the board, is often likened to a marriage that can last 10 years or more. As with any such relationship, we won't always make the right choices, and it's better for everyone to call time when you realise you are not fully compatible. Why compromise?

# NON-PROFIT, PRIVATE OR PUBLIC?

There are many different kinds of organisations that employ boards that include NEDs and other types of part-time advisers. I wrote earlier about my reasoning for not taking any uncompensated roles in my first cohort. But the available roles in the non-profit and public sectors are not always pro bono in nature. I once attended a seminar on this topic and was told about a useful website that lists HM Government public appointments. At the time of writing, this site listed more than 30 such appointments, which I suspect is a lower amount than usual due to Covid-19 restrictions at the time of writing (UK Lockdown 3.0). Each of these roles was compensated to some degree. I checked vacancies on this site from time-to-time, but nothing ever quite struck a chord with me. But your experience will be different.

The other big decision that I deliberated on was whether to join a publicly-traded company; most likely an AIM-listed PLC here in the UK. At the start of my transition, I was adamant that I would not. I applied the same reasoning that I had used during my executive career: people I knew that held senior leadership (officer) positions in public companies often lamented how much of their time was consumed by the overhead of managing public scrutiny (say investor relations), following heavy compliance and regulation regimes, attending committee meetings and so forth. This never appealed to me, a bit like with excessively long commutes. For me, the upsides (usually higher compensation) never outweighed this potential downside.

I sought advice from my network and mentors on making this decision and heard strong arguments both for and against joining public boards. In the end, the best piece of advice I received was: if you don't try it, how will you ever know? Furthermore, if you are good at it, and build a solid reputation, then this whole additional market is open to you in the future. Sounded logical to me. I was introduced to a few opportunities through some investors that straddled both the private and public markets and, whilst I found some exciting businesses, I still couldn't quite get myself over the line. I think, on reflection, that my passion for helping to scale early-stage companies was just not being fuelled by these, typically, later-stage businesses that had already floated on the public markets. Perhaps I will revisit this decision in the future, but for now all of the companies in my portfolio are privately held. Who knows, perhaps my first taste of PLC life will be when we take one of these to IPO.

## WHEN TO SAY NO THANK YOU

The other kind of business that I was keen to add to my portfolio was a for-profit, social purpose enterprise. A kind of half-way house between pure capitalism and doing good. Through a connection in the INSEAD alumni network, I was introduced to a fascinating business called Switchee that happened to be located just a stone's throw from my home in London's burgeoning knowledge quarter of Kings Cross.

Switchee is on a mission to improve the lives of people living in rented accommodation, especially those in social housing where fuel poverty is on the rise. At first, they did this with a smart internet-connected thermostat, somewhat akin to what Google does with Nest in the private (read more affluent) sector. They have a compelling future vision of the ultimate connected hub for the affordable home, which will further benefit residents and landlords alike.

I spent many happy hours discussing the business with the founders Adam Fudakowski and Ian Napier[5] and even went as far as meeting most of the board members and major investors with the view to joining them as chairman. We even got as far as hammering out the terms of my engagement, receiving an offer letter and then Adam and Ian kindly hand-delivering a bottle of champagne for us to celebrate my appointment. So why, in the final analysis, did I say no?

I must confess that this was a tough decision; my hardest choice thus far and not helped by a lingering regret that I can't team up with both Adam and Ian in the future. Some decisions are truly final. To set the context, I was evaluating a handful of chairman roles at the time and only had a couple of slots left to fill in my portfolio. Over that summer of 2019, I had to think long and hard about what I could really give to those remaining roles and how I would choose between them. The social purpose of the Switchee mission is a compelling one, and we could take pride in reducing fuel poverty whilst addressing a plethora of other issues that plague the social housing sector. It is easy to get excited about levelling up society.

My primary reservation was how much personal impact I could have on the business in the first 12 months. As a sales and marketing guy by trade, I am used to making an impact on revenue growth by skilling up teams that don't yet have senior commercial leaders in place. Switchee sells into the social housing sector, which has notoriously long sales cycles (measured in years) and where buying decisions are often aligned with refresh cycles based on maintenance and installation schedules; sending out engineers to install a new thermostat is feasible for a small pilot implementation but a full roll-out can take much longer. I figured that any positive impact that I could have on revenue growth might take one to two years to come to fruition.

Secondly, one of my first big tasks as the new chairman would have been to lead their next fund-raising effort. This is familiar territory for me; I have a well-developed and ever-growing investor network that streamlines the fundraising process based on my relationships and the trust between us. But a quick survey of the landscape told me that I did not know many of the impact investors that would most likely fit with the Switchee proposition. I felt that this would be a much greater effort for me than for some of the more mainstream B2B SaaS opportunities that I was also evaluating at that time (namely Scoro and Veeqo. which I did join). I was weighing up whether this was the most efficient use of my time and if I truly was the best person for the job. After much soul-searching, I decided that I was not the best person at that time.

I am pleased to say that my relationship with Adam continues to this day. We catch up over coffee from time to time and I gladly provide him with any help or advice I can with no expectation of receiving anything in return. I really want them to succeed in their mission to reduce fuel poverty. I was thrilled to learn that they recently closed the funding round that will enable them to reach the next level of product development and market penetration.

I also declined to pursue a few other opportunities around this time for more straightforward reasons, and with no regrets, so those stories are barely worth telling.

# CHEMISTRY IS KEY

I cannot overstate the importance of finding good chemistry from the start between a mentor and mentee. I consider it to be a privilege to go on the journey with these entrepreneurs, and the relationships are like marriages. Perhaps not so much pluralism as polygamy!

**NED NOTE:**

*"Chemistry is vital. I want to fall into a flow so whether you're agreeing or disagreeing, you're sparking off someone. And they're listening. Even if they're being robust, which I generally prefer, it's being done in the spirit of trying to understand the other point of view."*

By the time the founding team are ready to hire their first chairman – likely at Series A funding – they will have ground their way to ARR of more than £1m, which is hard to do. This means that entrepreneurs represent the tiny minority (less than1% of the population) that are willing and able to achieve such a milestone. It takes vast quantities of grit, vision and confidence to be a successful entrepreneur and, therefore, these individuals often have what I will politely term big personalities with demanding attitudes! Making an instant connection is certainly not assured and, particularly as an incoming chairman, you have to carefully consider the potential for developing a lasting and trustworthy relationship that will weather the many highs and lows along the journey. Building up this bank of personal equity is what gets you through the tough times.

### NED NOTE:

*"You need to find a willing partner. The best advice comes in the form of asking good questions, challenging the rigour of thought processes and sharing your experiences and networks. It doesn't mean having all of the answers."*

I believe that personal chemistry should come first on the list of selection criteria. So, I prefer to spend my first hour when evaluating a new opportunity just chatting with the founder(s) about them as people; shooting the breeze, as they say. The facts about the business, market opportunity, growth plans and so forth can all come later. In other words, I don't care how amazing the business opportunity sounds; if we don't click as people then the rest will be academic.

This is where traditional recruitment can get in the way unless the recruiter is both in tune and flexible. I am regularly approached by executive search firms, but I have only found one of my roles this way. My issue with recruiters is that they insist on getting to know you first – if they haven't placed you before – which invariably means an hour or two spent talking about yourself and the client brief rather than enjoying face time with the founders. On the flip side, I understand that it's the job of the recruiter to get in between the client and the candidate, because clients want to be protected from all candidates – except the one they hire. The best recruiters know when the right time is to step out of the way. I have found that Partner-led boutiques are savvier in this regard than large firms with their layers of personnel.

I appreciate why the recruitment industry has to work this way, but frankly it doesn't really work all that well for me as I get easily frustrated by the to-and-fro. If I were offering advice to the industry – specifically when it comes to handling non-executive search assignments – it would be to get out of the way as early in the process as possible. A well-written client brief plus a 30-minute phone call and some extensive background checking ought to suffice before introducing a candidate to the client. An alternative would be to use a digital recruitment platform like Nurole which has been specifically optimised for hiring board-level talent and is well-suited to the non-executive search process.

Nurole is one of the few platforms where I am registered as a candidate and where I accept weekly email notifications of new roles. Of course, I receive lots of in-bound opportunities via LinkedIn, but I never look there for roles. As most of my roles come via my network, I have still only found one position via Nurole

– despite my enthusiasm for the platform – but I must say that the candidate experience was excellent, and I much prefer their digital-first approach. I also hear good things from hiring companies (not least being the cost savings when compared with traditional search fees) and I know that the investor circle is also increasingly turning to Nurole as their platform of choice. They have certainly found a niche in the hyper-competitive UK recruitment market.

If you want to read more about my experience, then I granted a rare interview to Nurole which you can find here: Thinking of developing a NED portfolio career in the tech industry? Software entrepreneur Martin Fincham has these tips: https://www.nurole.com/news_and_guides/martin-fincham-chair-veeqo

# FUNDRAISING

This is not a chapter about how to raise money for early-stage companies. That topic has been well covered in published literature and blogs. What I want to address here are the expectations that will be put upon you as a board director – and especially as a chairman – when it comes to leading funding rounds for your portfolio companies. It's a skillset to be learned and then mastered.

Many people tell me that they dislike the fundraising process. But then most people dislike selling as well, and fundraising is just selling where the product is an equity shareholding in a company. Personally, I love selling and, regardless of the various job titles that I have carried over the years, I identify first and foremost as a software salesman. I suppose that my sales experience is more applicable to mastering the fundraising process than, say, being an engineer, so perfecting this craft may have been easier for me than it will be for you. My only advice is that if you are not already comfortable with pitching to strangers, and then running a sales process, then start practising now! Like I say about learning to play golf or tennis, it simply can't be done by reading books and watching a few training videos. You have to hit thousands of balls and always keep your hand in, even when you get to be good at it.

How to best pitch an investment proposition is also well-documented on the internet; there are many guides, templates and even real-world examples of winning decks out there. Notwithstanding all of this guidance, I rarely find that the draft of a pitch deck is as clear, concise and compelling as it needs to be to grab a jaded investor's attention and stimulate their interest to know more. Investors expect that you will cover a handful of key topics (the pain, evidence of demand, your solution, market sizing, the team, why now, the ask etc). Be sure to always hit these notes and have the conviction to be precise with your answers. Less is more.

As Woodrow Wilson once said: "If I am to speak for ten minutes, then I need a week for preparation; … if for an hour, then I am ready now." In other words, it is much easier to waffle.

I always ask people: what do you want me to *remember* about you? Human memory decays at an alarming rate and therefore I can remember much less after five days than after five minutes.

As an investor, when I make my decision whether to proceed to the next stage in the process (say at an investment committee meeting), what will I remember about you and your proposition and how will I communicate the highlights to my colleagues? If I start using your phraseology, then you did a good job on the communicating part. Along with choosing your words carefully, you must also have a firm grasp of the numbers; this is particularly true in SaaS where everything is expressed as a metric. Everyone on the pitch team, including non-execs, should be singing from the same hymn sheet. Investors despise ambiguity and inconsistency.

How else can you, as a NED, help with the fundraising process and make a strong first impression? Alongside bringing the power of your network to bear, I've found that a willingness to invest my own money is the most powerful differentiator. Self-explanatory really. As a rule, I only pitch deals to my investor network where I have already invested and/or intend to invest in this round and on the same terms as the incoming lead investor. Other intermediaries, like brokers, are typically not investing their own money and, moreover, are charging their client a success fee, so the motivations are different and not well aligned in my opinion. At the time of writing, I have raised tens of millions of pounds for my portfolio companies without using intermediaries or paying any success fees; including to myself. This work is all part of the job for which you are receiving your annual NED fee.

Once the term sheets start flying in, you will find that your focus is then helping the founders to choose. This evaluation consists of identifying the best fit 'partner' and negotiating the best terms. You will add more value at this stage as your portfolio grows and you have a handful of successful funding rounds under your belt. I could write a whole chapter on negotiating term sheets – and perhaps I will do a deep-dive in my next book – but suffice to say that once your experience is apparent to the potential investor, then two things will magically happen.

The first term sheet will have better terms because they know you are not naïve and thus easily exploited. Then the negotiation phase will be easier and faster because both parties know what 'market normal' looks like at that time. It also helps to understand their 'house style', which will become apparent once you have worked with the same investor a few times. You will also soon learn about the relationship between price (valuation) and terms (structure). As the saying goes, if given the choice between setting the price or the terms, then always choose to control the terms as then you can make virtually any price work for you. This correlation is often counter-intuitive to founders. They usually fixate on the price and don't always appreciate the potentially onerous nature of the terms that the investor has inserted to provide themselves with an appropriate level of control and downside protection. Cap tables and the waterfall models of how future distributions are made under certain scenarios can get really complicated.

These insights that you gain, and your ability to expedite the closing process once a term sheet has been agreed, are extremely valuable to the founders that you represent. You will also learn how to best guide them on the funding journey, as most start-ups require several rounds of capital before they reach break-down or find a buyer. Anticipating the arc of this journey is essential to optimising the shape and size of each round. It is not uncommon to find that future fundraising endeavours are hampered, or even blocked, by bad decisions made during the prior round. This is especially true when it comes to setting the price. An over-inflated early valuation can leave little wriggle room for execution missteps (leading to unpalatable flat or down rounds thereafter), and even later stage valuations that get excessively high will limit the universe of potential acquirers because there simply isn't enough headroom left in the market opportunity for them to generate their expected returns from the deal.

As your round enters the closing phase – having passed due diligence and the draft legals are going back and forth between those expensive lawyers – the board can best serve the executive team by helping to minimise the amount of legal work (potentially saving tens of thousands of pounds). Such help comes in the form of starting with good heads of terms, having anticipated and addressed all of the typically thorny issues, knowing how to streamline the process (read as not being taken advantage of when it comes to billings) and insisting on working with the best people in those law firms who simply get stuff done.

Once the legals are all but finished, the board can work with the management team on drawing-up the outline of a 100-day post-investment plan. In my experience, sophisticated investors will insist on having such a plan in place. Many of the actions in the plan will be remedial issues identified during the due diligence process, but the plan should not become one-sided. What specific requests will the company make of the new investor? If they are truly a value-added investor, then they should be able to help with leadership development, hiring new executive talent, opening doors to prospective customers and partners, introducing peers from their other portfolio companies to compare notes on go-to-market strategies and tactics, bridging across oceans and so forth.

# GETTING PAID

It's OK if you jumped straight to this section of the book – I would have done the same! Remuneration setting is the one aspect of going plural that I found to be most opaque when I started out. Fortunately, since then, market research reports have been published that cover the basics and provide some good benchmark data for fairly negotiating your terms of engagement. It is much harder to find a mutually acceptable deal when starting expectations are mismatched. Benchmarks help both parties to feel assured that they struck a good bargain, and this positive strength of feeling is important when you consider the type of intimate work that you will be doing together over potentially many years.

The executive search firm Spectrum publish a report entitled 'The role of the Board Chair within privately held growth businesses' which can be downloaded from their website: https://spectrum-ehcs.com.

The introduction to this report reads as follows: "Before the collapse of Lehman Brothers, we had not been asked to conduct a Board search. Afterwards, we were. This was initially driven by investors who wanted to de-risk and better understand their portfolio companies. And, in more recent years, Board Chair recruitment has equally been driven by founding management teams who wanted the experience, advice and mentorship that an appropriate Non-Executive Chair could offer them.

"However, the emergence of the Board Chair role is still relatively new in smaller, private businesses. There is little in the way of formal training, and although there are some publications that have sought to explore the role in earlier-stage businesses, we have not found any guides that have been research based.

"So, we undertook a survey of Non-Executive Chairs to establish their views and experiences. And, as stakeholder alignment is everything, we also asked Investors, and CEOs, to provide their views on the Board Chair role. We are grateful to the 95 board members who completed surveys (45 Board Chairs, 27 Investors, 23 CEOs) as their feedback forms the core of this report."

The report includes more insights than simply revealing compensation data, but in this regard I have found the benchmark data to be very useful. The data set covers time commitments, reward mix, day rates, stock allocations and so forth. I consider this report to be essential reading for candidates, companies and investors.

The second source of research that I recommend is the Nurole Independent Director Compensation Survey which can be downloaded from their website: www.nurole.com

This survey is broader in nature as the scope is board compensation from 600 organisations, ranging from start-up to Fortune 500, and it covers all independent director roles, not just that of chairman. Their data set includes:

- Total remuneration and day rates.
- Average days spent on the roles.
- Investment requirements and percentage ownership.
- Number of positions held.

Not having the benefit of this market research when I started out, I applied the simple approach of setting myself a target amount for a blended day rate once the portfolio was fully built. I took my steer from the consulting industry where I had some legacy knowledge from having sold technical consultancy (software developers, architects, project managers) in my past and also from professional advisors that I had hired from time to time during my career. I anticipated there being four acceptable price points:

- Seed stage companies (likely founder/family/angel funded).
- Start-ups (post first institutional investment, say Series A).
- Scale-ups (say post Series B).
- Super scale-ups/turnarounds (likely backed by private equity).

I have found this anticipated price elasticity to be true and, by mixing the right blend of roles, have achieved my initial blended day rate from which, hopefully, the only way is up.

However, when I say day rate, this is actually a misnomer. Whilst the concept of a 'day rate' is a unit of measure that both parties can easily grasp, it does not always correlate well with the duties and expectations of the role. Each and every week I simply do whatever it takes to help my companies to succeed. I do not keep a record of the time that I spend with each company. Even the frequency of my board meetings varies between companies, from six to 12 times per year. There will be peaks of activity, around say fund-raising, crisis management and exits, where the load can easily rise by threefold for a sustained period (months). There are even periods of calm when I sometimes feel that I am not contributing enough and ask if there are any special projects I can help with.

Where I do find it really helps to anticipate 'days spent' on the job is in planning your work schedule to ensure that you have not over-extended yourself in terms of business commitments or compromising your work/life balance goal. I initially set my work/life balance goal at 50:50, giving me 10 working days per month to spend as a NED. A chairman role will likely take up two to three days per month, whereas a regular NED role is usually just one day per month for board meeting preparation, attendance and follow-up.

Applying these assumptions to your desired number of working days will enable you to calculate the type and total quantity of roles that is optimal for your portfolio. Note that I have since exceeded my original 50:50 target because I am having too much fun with my portfolio companies!

There is a danger of taking on too much work because, whilst it is arguably easier to drop NED roles than full-time executive jobs, I do believe that each commitment should be for the whole journey if the board so desires. Personally, I would not want to develop a reputation for being flighty. On the other hand, I know investors that see value in rotating board members on a regular basis (every year or two), so there is definitely more flexibility in the non-executive world and potentially less damage inflicted on your CV in hopping around – providing that you meet the board's expectations every time. The UK technology scene can feel like a small world, especially inside of the London bubble, and reputations spread very quickly – for better and for worse.

When it comes to receiving your cash compensation in the most tax-efficient way, the choices have shrunk in recent years whereby, in the UK at least, the tax collector (HMRC) now expects that companies process such fees through payroll (PAYE) like for any other employee. In the past, and before my time, there were alternatives like forming a personal services company through which to invoice for your fees. I understand that the advantages would have included offsetting certain allowable expenses and taking the profits as dividend payments, which used to attract a lower rate of income tax. However, all of my UK sourced income for NED work is processed through company payrolls. In addition, I am a partner in The Gorilla Factory LLP, along with my wife, Joanna, as we bill for our ad-hoc consultancy work by invoicing our clients. I don't do much ad-hoc consultancy work anymore (and only usually as special projects for my portfolio companies) but Joanna does as she offers strategic marketing consultancy services to technology start-ups and scale-ups. The LLP is VAT registered in the UK, as our turnover exceeds the required threshold, so this is helpful in reclaiming the VAT on larger purchases like new equipment.

To my mind, the main financial upside of being plural is the opportunity to make multiple investments in high-potential companies where such equity is not usually offered to the general public because of the risks involved. Therefore, as previously mentioned, be prepared to invest in each company and, even when not required, why wouldn't you? These investment opportunities are particularly attractive when they qualify for tax relief in the form of the UK's SEIS and EIS schemes and are held for the minimum term (currently three years). When I look back one day, and do my final tally, I expect the vast majority of the financial gains to have come from returns on these investments and not from the more heavily taxed cash compensation or stock options.

Having said that, I also expect to receive a stock option grant along with the equity that I invest. This is normal practice, according to the research I've highlighted, so I am not unusual in this regard. The market research reports will guide you on the reasonable ranges to expect depending on the stage of the company. For any special situations, I have found that calculating the size of the stock option grant as a multiple of your investment to be an equitable solution e.g. 3 options granted for every 1 share purchased. I believe that it is healthy to have everyone aligned around stock option value growth – from the chairman down to the next junior hire.

Of course, the downside of receiving stock options, at least in the UK, is that you are ultimately taxed on the gains at the highest rate of income tax (exceeding 50% in most circumstances). Whilst full-time employees can benefit from approved tax-advantage schemes – like the Enterprise Management Incentive (EMI) scheme – alas part-time employees, like NEDs, do not qualify and therefore can only receive so-called unapproved options. Your tax advisor can discuss the pros and cons of other structures with you that may be more tax advantageous depending on the circumstances, such as reverse vesting and growth shares. I have found David Marcussen of Marcussen Consulting to be very knowledgeable in such matters.

In summary, you can establish a C-suite level of income (if that is what you are used to receiving) from the sum of the fees for performing six to eight non-executive roles. But my blunt advice is that the fun factor and potential equity gains are better motivators than simply the income.

# RUNNING AN EFFECTIVE BOARD

There are many books published on this topic – in fact, I'm reading *Boards: A Practical Perspective* by Patrick Dunne as I write this chapter – so I won't attempt to repeat that in-depth literature here. Instead, I will share a few perspectives and practical learnings with you.

A board is only truly useful in helping the CEO and the team manage their business if the board itself is well managed. There are several truisms that I've found with early-stage businesses:

1. Incoming NEDs assume that the CEO knows how to run board meetings effectively.
2. CEOs assume that board directors expect them to simply report on their performance and progress.

One of my first tasks as incoming chair is to reset these expectations so the management team becomes aware of what a good board pack looks like. I then coach them, month-by-month, until we have found the right balance for them and the stage of their business. There is no one-size-fits-all format here, and I believe it is important to keep individual personalities and preferences in mind. Whilst each of the seven boards on which I current sit operate within the bounds of normal practice, they are each distinct in their group dynamic, and in where we place certain points of emphasis at any given moment of time. I am comfortable waiting up to six months for a new board to find its grove, although this could easily happen after just three months of iterations. No less than once per year, the format and frequency of board meetings should be reviewed by the CEO and chairman to ensure they are still fit for purpose. It would also be considered best practice to review the composition of the board on an annual basis, along with conducting formal performance reviews with each board member. I must confess that such formality is rare, and likely overkill, with start-up companies but is becoming increasingly commonplace as we scale (say more than £5m ARR in a B2B SaaS business).

In terms of distributing the board pack, it is essential that members receive the data in sufficient time to process and formulate questions before the meeting. Some boards encourage that routine questions (usually about the financial and performance data) be asked by email in advance such that the in-person meeting time can be reserved for more valuable discussions. The three pillars of appropriate board content are strategy, reporting and leadership.

The strategy work is what it sounds like – elevating the conversation higher than simply reporting on current trading performance and day-to-day issues by anticipating what lurks around the next big corner; be those opportunities or threats. The collective wisdom of experienced board members can illuminate many dark corners. I describe the scale-up journey as being different from the start-up phase because of the multi-dimensional nature of choice and necessity.

Start-ups, whilst agonisingly difficult to launch and grow, are relatively simple beasts to manage when you are in survival mode. But as you scale the business, the challenges go from a two-dimensional problem (usually single product/single market) to more of a three-dimensional puzzle that requires managing complex teams handling multiple products/variants serving multiple markets (geographies) and addressing multiple vertical industries.

You will find that topics like product roadmap prioritisation, market positioning, distribution channels, competition, hiring and talent development, strategic partnerships and fundraising require constant attention and revisitation. I encourage my CEOs to bring forward at least one big strategy question to every meeting. This is where the non-operational nature of NEDs brings valuable perspective and, if the composition is correct, they should have the relevant experience to help avoid most pitfalls and the professional networks to fast-track the introductions that will accelerate progress.

Board time is extremely valuable – just see how hard it is to get everybody in the same room and keep them focused and engaged. Do not make the classic mistake of spending too much time on reporting, even though this is often how start-ups think that board meetings will run. Much of the reporting burden can happen outside of the room. It is not uncommon for me to find that my first board meeting consists almost exclusively of the founder(s) reading bullet points from the slide deck in the pack. Here you have an incredible pool of talent at your disposal, and you choose to use the time firing bullet points at them?

The third pillar of board-appropriate content is leadership. The board can help founders to become better leaders, and also support their leadership of the team in board meetings themselves. Founders should bring members of their team in for different parts of a meeting.

From a NED perspective, nothing beats having the sales leader give their nuanced judgement of the sales pipeline; or when the head of product demos a killer enhancement with the passion that only an owner can muster. It's even fun watching the CFO squirm as we test cash-flow assumptions to within an inch of their life! These experiences are good for sharing the expertise of your team across your board (and vice-versa), and these are also critical one-to-one relationships to establish - especially for a chairman that seeks to provide operational expertise outside of the boardroom.

Bringing the leadership team into the room (or Zoom conference) will be motivating to them and sharpen their performance, as presentations to the board are usually considered to be the gold standard. Board meeting dates also serve as useful deadlines for finishing off pesky tasks and written plans. A great board meeting is a working meeting and such inclusion will also demonstrate transparency, expose the team to other aspects of the business and allow credit to be earned and recognised by the board. I always value seeing the team in action, watching them sparking off each other and collaborating on shared goals. Such insight is far more valuable than simply having them report on just their own responsibilities. Long-form strategy days (off-site) make for great additions to the annual calendar and allow for more free-flowing discussions than can be crammed into short-form board meetings. Longer sessions are when board members can really feel the cohesion of a team, whilst experiencing more of the culture (ways of working) and thereby adapting their behaviour to best fit with the team dynamic. Hosting a few dinners and drink sessions also goes a long way to galvanising everyone into one team - avoiding the toxic trap of a 'them' (board) versus 'us' (management) syndrome, which will only harm the chances for mutual success.

Great boards can make – and bad boards can break – a fast-growing business. First-time founders often overlook the importance of deliberately constructing a board. Their boards are usually heavy with investor representation and they can feel stuck with representatives they are given rather than ones they've chosen. Whilst there are naturally some limits to the composition (based on investor rights), an independent chairman will add great value by getting the right people on the bus, the wrong people off the bus and helping to keep the bus heading in the right direction, and at the right speed.

Let's dig into both the independence and diversity topics. Apparently, from Silicon Valley to Europe, independent board members still remain the exception. I read some research suggesting that only a quarter of start-ups employ independent directors, and this stat fits with my anecdotal evidence. By definition, board members should have the company's best interests at heart. But all too often, investors are thinking about their return on investment and can find themselves conflicted when the big moments come - like whether to accept an acquisition offer or not.

Seeking independent advice is critical – to deepen perspectives and find new ones; for conflict resolution and building bridges; for mentoring; and, most importantly, to ensure a diverse set of viewpoints are represented. Bringing diverse and independent opinions into the room is an effective remedy against biased and rash decision-making. Diversity is not only about gender; it goes far beyond, addressing age, ethnicity, background, experience, industry and sexual orientation. I must confess that, thus far, I have joined predominately "male and pale" boards, and so increasing diversity is high on my to-do list.

From a personality perspective, the best NEDs are those who are clear on their "nose-in, hands-out role" as a board member, who proactively engage with the industry related to their portfolio to remain current (not resting on past laurels), and who conduct themselves with empathy and professionalism in equal measure.

In summary, the best boards are a natural extension of the management team, and they should make the CEO, team and company perform better at every distinct stage in the company's growth. Communication should be frequent and easy – natural if you will – and never feel like an onerous burden. The board should only request data that is truly insightful and supports their decision-making, not requesting information for the sake of being curious or, worse, a busybody. I am acutely aware of just how much work is required, every month, to produce seemingly simple

KPIs, and therefore the chairman must remain vigilant that the management team is not being stressed unnecessarily.

## Top 10 Tips for Operating an Effective Board

1. Having four to seven members is ideal. Don't engineer for political balance or try to optimise for odd and even numbers.

2. Early-stage boards should meet six to 10 times per year. Post-pandemic, it seems that alternating between in-person and remote will be normal and more efficient.

3. Board meetings should be two to four hours long; all day meetings should be avoided, but lunches/dinners are helpful for bonding and building up personal equity.

4. Does the board feel like a team that was formed to help the company? More importantly, does the CEO agree with this?

5. Have targets for introducing, and maintaining, sufficient diversity of thought.

6. Consider adding at least one industry non-exec and rotating that position frequently as business needs evolve.

7. Spend more than half of the board meeting discussing strategic topics. Preparation and focus are key to minimising the debilitating effect of posturing and filibustering.

8. You can iterate KPIs and reporting formats but stick to them for at least 12 months else year-on-year comparisons become meaningless. Quarterly views help you to see around monthly corners.

9. CEO and CFO presence are mandatory, but also consider giving airtime to other members of the leadership team on a rotating basis (and coach them well).

10. Manage burning issues outside of the board meeting as they materialise; there should be no surprises at the meeting.

# NEDS IN A CRISIS

E ven with the best crisis management plans at hand, nobody could have predicted the Covid-19 pandemic that befell the world in 2020 and turned the global economy on its head. Just before putting pen to paper on this book, I was invited to participate on a panel with a handful of other experienced NEDs to learn how we handled uncertainty within our businesses, our shifting role during the pandemic, and the positive changes that came as a result.

This virtual event was facilitated by my good friend Jonathan McKay, who was my inspiration for going plural and a mentor without whom my transition would have been far more haphazard. Jonathan was ably assisted by Eyal Malinger (investment director at Beringea) and hosted by the 'chairman and NED' practice of the rather excellent search firm, La Fosse Associates.

## How Did NEDs React Immediately After the Pandemic Broke?

Most attendees agreed that pre-emptive board meetings began around February, with contingency, or 'drawer', plans around home-working capability and other crisis management procedures being top of the agenda. Investors also took time to review their portfolio companies and the impact that the pandemic might have on each business.

With a universal 'fog of war' around what would happen over the coming months, and massive levels of fear and uncertainty across the globe, hyper-communication became a key tactic in staying on top of things as they developed. A lot of the NEDs said they were engaged in weekly calls with CEOs, discussing everything from mental wellbeing to identifying industry experts to assist in proceedings. Risk committees and registers also came to the fore, allowing businesses of all sizes to plan for the changing environment and look at overall risk.

As revenue and share prices plummeted in the public markets, and with detailed scenario planning practically impossible, focus switched to cash conservation. Within their portfolio companies, NEDs moved into triage mode, asking questions such as:

1. Who's likely to be suffering?
2. Who won't be heavily impacted?
3. Who will benefit?

Existing preparatory measures also varied greatly depending on the size of the business. With such a fast-hitting wave, a lot of smaller companies had not had the bandwidth to make contingency plans, and as such were completely unprepared for the effects of the pandemic. As one fellow NED noted, a lot of start-up founders are domain or tech experts, as opposed to businesspeople, so having an experienced NED on board was crucial. For me this was my fifth recession. For many early-stage businesses, the primary focus was on cutting burn rather than fundraising, although some did benefit from the latter.

Even within bigger organisations, there was still a general sense of unpreparedness and denial during the early weeks. The first port of call for many was to ensure two key things:

- Business continuity.
- Employee protection (safety and security).

In an environment where the spread of outcomes was so large, decisions had to be quick, but flexible, to allow optimal adaptivity. Good preparation, sensible control metrics, a care for the people and, ultimately, the cooperation and availability of board members were all key in surviving the first couple of months.

## How Has the Role of the NED Shifted During the Pandemic?

Never before have boards been so valuable and had to make big decisions this quickly. With no time to reflect, the nature of the NED role (especially in the early months) shifted dramatically from being led by instinct rather than experience, as an 'all-hands-on-deck' mentality emerged.

In some businesses with inexperienced boards, it fell to NEDs to steer the company through this tumultuous period. As one NED asserted:

*"In some early-stage businesses with inexperienced or entrepreneurial creative execs, we consciously overstepped our NED role because people were paralysed with fear of the business not surviving. With senior teams being nervous about furlough and redundancy, we stepped in appropriately to drive decisions, something which I saw as inevitable."*

In others, NED involvement was on a sliding scale. From normalising trading levels and securing investments to simply overseeing other responsibilities like hiring in order to give executives the space to get the job done, many NEDs played some role in stabilising businesses before consciously stepping further back in later months.

In any case, having a NED on board was a key advantage for providing an external perspective based on how other portfolio companies were responding, while allowing executives to focus on internal operations.

## How Did 'Remote-Only' Change Our Ways of Working?
Benefits:
- On the whole, young teams have been much quicker to adapt to new communication tools and have shown increased agility by taking challenges in their stride and seeing them as a learning opportunity. As one fellow NED noted: "Never let a good crisis go to waste!"

- Some leaders have reconsidered their whole business plans since working from home, realising that they would rather not waste time and money on travel.

Challenges:
- Recruitment over Zoom is quick and easy, but the challenge is onboarding, as it's hard to tell if people are fully understanding and engaging or not. As such, one portfolio company reportedly changed their probation process and became more vivid (and explicit) with KPIs to gain an understanding of what 'good' looks like in this new environment.
- With an increased reliance on contribution over personality, companies have had to shift from visibility management to output management as they reconsider how to best measure performance.
- For companies who have relied on face-to-face sales meetings (especially internationally), this new sterile sales environment has made it difficult to get the attention of new clients. People are suffering from Zoom fatigue, resulting in a lack of focus and depth to conversations.

## Did Working from Traditional Metrics Make Sense Anymore?

Where we have had to adjust budgets in flight, they've been very reactive and based upon very little true trajectory or path.

The increased amount of forecasting and re-forecasting amidst so much uncertainty has left finance professionals with perpetually outdated budgets. Some businesses have adopted a multi-level budget approach based on best- and worst-case scenarios, re-fore-casting every month to review recent changes, which has required some NEDs to become more focused and confident with numbers.

Under usual circumstances, leadership teams work on output metrics when planning ahead, rather than during heads-down execution mode. With that path not available, many NEDs found themselves focusing conversations around how to base models on organisational drivers in order to make forecasting easier. Without knowing when sales momentum will return, the concept of under-standing the cost drivers of your business, and then where to put investment, is both crucial and much less complex than making decisions based on the present moment.

Staff can also get paralysed and believe that they are not performing well, or that things are much worse than they actually are, so it's the role of the NED to highlight the positives and provide reassurance to the executive team.

## What Changes Might Now Be Permanent?

- **Transition to cash and cost management instead of profit and loss management** – more focus on what we're spending on and why. Capital-efficient growth rules over growth at any cost.
- **Frequent, transparent and open communications with stakeholders** – being 'forced' into increased communica-tion with regulators and suppliers over the past year has resulted in a lot of learning, better relationships and more conversations around future opportunities.

- **Enabling small companies to continue with discovering product market fit** – in a lot of cases this year, angel investors have got on board to help start-ups capture opportunities and turn them into better prospects for raising funds from institutional investors.

## Key Takeaways about Crisis Management Amidst the Pandemic

- Hyper-communication is key.
- React fast, cut burn and decide which market you're really in.
- Boards are compelled to act and learn a lot as a result.
- Scenario planning and unexpected outcomes were both positive and negative.
- Talented leadership focuses on developing and executing continuity plans.
- Building flood defences now makes businesses stronger going forward.
- Young, inexperienced teams can be more reactive and shift faster than older teams.

Writing this now, in February 2021, with the benefit of 12 months of hindsight, I can confidently attest that this was the most tumultuous, and yet curiously rewarding, period of my career. I worked full-time from 16th March, 2020 through to the not-really-Xmas break in December.

Being a NED was no longer a part-time job. Being a NED was no longer about attending regular board meetings. Being a NED meant becoming the co-pilot to everyone that needed help in the cockpit. I feel that, for an ex-operator like me, this was a natural reaction and, besides, what else was there to do except roll-up your sleeves and avoid daytime television at all costs? It would be premature to attempt to draw this chapter to a close, as we are unfortunately not yet out of the pandemic phase. The health crisis is still very real, and thus the full extent of the existing economic crisis is yet to be fully realised. On the positive side, vaccinations in Britain have just passed the 20m mark and spring has sprung with hope of a more normal summer. So I will save further musings on this topic for the start of my next book. By then, I hope that we will be well into the new-normal, with this horrendous human tragedy behind us and the world learning how to cope with an endemic virus.

## The Future Fund

For posterity, I wish to record what an effective intervention the Government made during the 'fog of war' that descended during the most fearful and panic-inducing moments of the pandemic (May 2020). I still shudder when I think back to nightly news bulletins of Italian hospitals overflowing with the sick and death rates skyrocketing at home and abroad.

The £500m Future Fund was launched to support innovative and high-growth British businesses needing to secure investment to help them through the Coronavirus outbreak. Private investors – potentially including venture capital funds, angel investors like myself and those backed by regional funds – would at least match the Government investment in these companies.

The Chancellor of the Exchequer, Rishi Sunak, said:

*"Our start-ups and innovative firms are one of our great economic strengths, and they will help spur our recovery from the pandemic. The Future Fund will support firms across the UK to get through the pandemic by stimulating investment, so that they can continue to break new ground in technology and innovation."*

Furthermore, match fund investors were encouraged to sign the Treasury's Investing in Women Code, which commits firms to improving female entrepreneurs' access to tools, resources and finance. The Future Fund was a signatory of this.

By the time the fund closed to new applications (January 2021), £1.12bn of investment had been unlocked via convertible loans for 1,140 companies, displaying an admirable spread of diversity:

- 39% of funding to companies outside London, worth £438.7m.
- 78% of funding to mixed gender senior management teams.
- 57% of funding to mixed ethnicity senior management teams.

There were 1,846 applications in total since the launch, which means that more than 60% of applicants were successful in raising, on average, £1m per company. I shudder to think how many socially progressive high-tech jobs would have been lost without this intervention; not to mention the catastrophic effect on a post-Brexit Britain of losing so many high-potential growth companies.

It's not often that you will find me celebrating the Government for their business-friendly policies, but the Future Fund, along with continued operation of the EIS/SEIS tax relief schemes, deserves all the applause. I sincerely hope that the UK Treasury receives significant future returns on these investments to demonstrate that such interventions are in the national interest and don't actually cost taxpayers any money. I also give a special commendation to the British Business Bank, which brought this, and other schemes, to life in record time and ran a fully-remote, straightforward process under testing conditions (like 100% work from home).

It only made sense for one of my portfolio companies, BlackCurve, to raise a bridge round in late 2020. The others (like SHE Software) had either recently closed large rounds, had equity raises in process or simply didn't qualify for the scheme as they didn't have a UK-based headquarters. I led this round for BlackCurve and found the experience to be quicker and less arduous than many previous raises. Special thanks are given to my fellow angel investors, who rallied when many – quite understandably in the midst of a pandemic – had drawn in their horns. I was joined by fellow Cambridge Angels, prominent industry figures and ScaleUp Group members, with additional institutional investment coming from our lead investor Nauta Capital.

# MIND THE EXIT

As a lifelong salesman and sales leader, I am well used to being on both the giving and receiving end of the old adage: "You are only as good as your last sale!"

It's pretty much the same bar for a NED – especially a chairman: "You are only as good as your last exit." This expectation is particularly acute when your appointment has been sponsored by an investor. Given the relative youth of my current cohort, we have not yet sold any companies…albeit there may be some 'scores on the doors' by the end of 2021 as inbound interest is at an all-time high level. My portfolio companies have made some acquisitions, and this trend may well accelerate as, post-pandemic, there appears to be more sub-scale businesses that are buds just ready to blossom.

What I can share with you now is how I approach generating shareholder alignment when I first join the board (as chair) and, in addition, what several M&A deals have taught me about making best preparations to exit for a premium price. Not all companies are built to be sold, but as I work alongside financial investors, an exit is the goal for all of my current portfolio. It is often said that "great companies are brought, not sold", which is a euphemism for not optimising daily tasks for an exit, but rather to stay focused on building a great company which is held in high regard by all stakeholders. That being said, shareholder value can be easily destroyed, or at least constrained, by not knowing how to play the shareholder alignment and strategic premium games.

## Shareholder Alignment

In early-stage companies – with just one external investor – there is unlikely to be any misalignment around the opportunity ahead unless the founder(s) made a poor choice of their lead investor or there is a complex shareholder structure full of angels, family and friends. But once several institutional investors are on board – say post Series A – then it is vital for an incoming chair to run the following simple exercise.

I like to start with a survey to the major shareholders. The definition of major will vary, but usually this means shareholders with more than 10% of the equity and/or a seat on the board (or veto rights). My standard questions are:

1. What is your expected timeframe for exit?
2. What valuation would you expect to see?
3. What are the top three characteristics/achievements you think our company would need to demonstrate to achieve a premium exit valuation?
4. Who are the likely acquirers and why?

Short and sweet. You could no doubt think of more questions, but I find that investors have limited bandwidth and therefore I keep it simple for them. The answers I receive are sufficient for me to move to the next step, which is to draft a 'What Needs to be True?' matrix that is then discussed and filled in during a strategy session. An example for a B2B SaaS business looks like this:

| ATTRIBUTE | MEASUREMENT | YEAR 1 | YEAR 2 | YEAR 3 | EXIT HORIZON |
| | what to measure? | (funding £) | (funding £) | (funding £) | (valuation £) |
| --- | --- | --- | --- | --- | --- |
| Category Leader | Industry analyst positioning<br><br>- Gartner<br>- G2/Capterra/GetApp | \<blank\> | \<blank\> | \<blank\> | Desired industry placement and recognition by the opening of the exit window |
| >50% Growth YoY | - Subscription revenue<br>- ARR?<br>- Current MRR x 12? | \<blank\> | \<blank\> | \<blank\> | Target revenue threshold and three-year CAGR e.g. £10m ARR at 60% growth |
| Presence in North America | >50% of new orders? | \<blank\> | \<blank\> | \<blank\> | e.g. U.S. ARR greater than EMEA ARR |
| Product Superiority | Competitive win rate? | \<blank\> | \<blank\> | \<blank\> | e.g. CAC trending down for inbound |
| Net Dollar Retention | >120% | \<blank\> | \<blank\> | \<blank\> | e.g. 120%+ or whatever is best-in-class at the time |
| GTM Scalability | - Inbound vs. outbound split<br><br>- Channel mix – optimal? | \<blank\> | \<blank\> | \<blank\> | e.g. 60/20/20 split between inbound, outbound and channel |
| Strong Unit Economics | - CAC, payback<br>- Rule of 40<br>- Revenue per FTE<br>- EBITDA | \<blank\> | \<blank\> | \<blank\> | e.g. CAC:LTV > 3<br><br>Net MRR retention > 100% |

I find that this 'ready-reckoner' provides useful guidance when setting annual goals and reviewing performance; a simple method by which progress can be measured along the vectors that we believed at the start of the investment cycle will most likely lead to a premium exit. This matrix should be updated every year, usually at an off-site strategy day.

## Successful Exit Benchmarks

If the company appoints a sell-side adviser, like an accountancy firm or investment bank, then they will likely have their own scorecard for gauging how the performance of your company compares with its contemporaries. They will also find reasonable comparisons with similar publicly-traded companies, where all of their readily available financial performance data can be aggregated to set some upper-quartile benchmarks. Within these comparisons you will find the drivers that generate strategic value i.e. a premium price. The usual set of drivers always applies, but there will also be moment-in-time levers which can be pulled if the stars align. For example, in my world of B2B SaaS, the world currently looks like this:

1. The whole sector has proven to be surprisingly resilient during the Covid pandemic and is therefore trading at a premium to the broader economy (a relative safe haven if you will).

2. There is a wall of late-stage investment and acquisition capital that was dammed up during the pandemic and is

now being aggressively deployed; too much money chasing too few quality opportunities.

3. New acquirers – notably Special Purpose Acquisition Companies (SPACs) – are competing with the more traditional exit routes of private equity and regular IPOs.

4. Product-led growth (PLG) is a go-to-market strategy that is proving to generate better unit economics than traditional sales-led growth (SLG). PLG is an end user-focused model that relies on the product itself as the primary driver of customer acquisition, conversion and expansion. Not every company is ready, willing or able to adopt the PLG method. Those that have are being rewarded with a strategic premium. This trend is likely to persist for several years as the transition (from SLG) is not trivial, and native PLG start-ups are just becoming the majority but most are not yet at scale.

5. New technologies like artificial intelligence, machine learning and blockchain may have past their peak of the hype cycle – often causing eyes to roll when peppered throughout a start-up pitch deck – but traditional software vendors are increasingly augmenting their legacy portfolios with bolt-on product acquisitions and acqui-hires.

These forces are conspiring to drive up prices, and therefore it is a seller's market. Alongside these moment-in-time levers, the usual set of drivers are:

## 1. Scale of Opportunity

    a. Current Revenue: bracketed by buyer type e.g. PE enters at more than £10m ARR.

    b. Total Addressable Market: less of the blue-sky thinking of venture capital and more a question of how much growth is left in the market as the acquirer gauges their upside from here.

## 2. Business Model

    a. Recurring Revenue Percentage

    b. Gross Margin Percentage

    c. Annual Contract Value

## 3. Customer Retention

    a. Average Contract Length

    b. Churn Percentage (by value or by logo or both)

    c. Net Renewal Rate (the rate at which customers are renewing and expanding)

## 4. Sales Efficiency

    a. Quote Achievement Per Sales FTE (full-time equivalent)

    b. Customer Acquisition Cost (CAC)

    c. Lifetime Value (LTV) to CAC ratio

## 5. "Rule of 40"

    a. ARR Growth ("G")

    b. EBITDA Margin ("M")

c. Rule of 40 ("G+M"), where more than 40% is upper-quartile performance

In addition to helping the founder(s), leadership team, board and major shareholders think through all of the above, a chairman will really come into his/her own when helping to screen approaches by acquirers – there's a lot of tyre-kickers out there – and then finally running the M&A process.

## Chairman's Role During an Exit

It is better if the CEO is not the point-person on the deal. Firstly, they have to run the business and the process will become a real time sink; a bit like the laborious effort of fundraising, but on steroids. It is very easy to destroy shareholder value by inadvertently allowing business performance to suffer during an intense acquisition process. There is nothing that the acquirer likes better than being able to 'chip' the price down because you missed your targets! Also, it is likely that the CEO and senior leadership team will be expected to stay on post-acquisition; often tied in for up to three years with a retention package. This means that they have to work with the people the deal was negotiated with, and this can get awkward when the inevitable hard moments and choices come.

It is unlikely that the board will remain intact after an acquisition, and therefore the chairman, and any other NEDs, can play 'bad cop' without fear or favour as well as providing invaluable deal support and guidance. They are likely to have more experience of selling than the founding team and can therefore remain calm under pressure and know what good, bad and market-average terms look like. NEDs should expect to work considerably harder (more hours) during this process and therefore should remain conscious of their availability. If the acquirer is foreign, then, say, an eight-hour difference of time zone will compound your deal fatigue. When you have a large portfolio, like me, it is essential to start planning every hour of every day to ensure that you remain responsive to the dynamics of the deal but, as importantly, to protect other service levels and meet your commitments elsewhere.

Whilst being buffeted by the powerful forces of founders and lead investors – not to mention the armies of lawyers and other advisors – someone needs to represent and safeguard the interests of minority shareholders that don't have a seat at the table and will be 'dragged' to sell their shares. As chairman, you are the most senior independent director and therefore best positioned to represent all stakeholders, including customers, suppliers, employees and the community e.g. keeping employment in the home town.

I expect that if/when I write a second book, I will have more hard-earned battle scars, top tips and war stories to share. At the moment my portfolio is in rude health with credible exit plans and expectations across the board. Let's see how this cohort plays out.

# ABOUT THE AUTHOR

After a 30-year career in the technology business, as both an entre-preneur and corporate CEO, I now enjoy a pluralist portfolio life. I am regarded by fellow board members as an expert on both setting the most effective go-to-market strategy and for delivering operational excellence in the modern B2B sales environment.

My functional skills include B2B sales, marketing and growth management. I have, for a commercial guy, unusually deep technical expertise, having trained as both a software and hardware engineer, allowing me to talk straight with engineering teams and to connect with brilliant technical founders.

My experience ranges from having founded my own software company aged 24, to selling it for a lucrative amount and then working in Silicon Valley for five years, to more recently being

CEO of a global software vendor where I increased EBITDA by seven-fold during my tenure. I am an ex-board member and current associate of the Cambridge Angels Network.

**www.gorillafactory.co.uk**
**www.linkedin.com/in/martinfincham**

# Endnotes

1 Fred was a prominent, long-time Silicon Valley public relations and marketing executive. He was vice president of communications for Apple Computer, where he was involved with the company's initial public offering and the product launches of the Lisa and Macintosh computers. I met him as chairman and head of technology practice at Miller/Shandwick, which was our PR agency.

2 Source: https://www.linkedin.com/posts/foundersfactory_startups-ai-design-activity-6763379977099468800-ESA6

3 A Commander (ENTJ) is someone with the Extroverted, Intuitive, Thinking, and Judging personality traits. They are decisive people who love momentum and accomplishment. They gather information to construct their creative visions but rarely hesitate for long before acting on them. This sounds a lot more like me than my horoscope version!

4 If you read up to this point, rather than simply flicking straight to this chapter, then you will have deduced that this person is John Yeomans of Wazoku.

5 Tragically, less than six months later, Ian became a victim of another rising threat in modern society – male suicide. I regret not having taken the opportunity to work alongside this brilliant and passionate man. Adam has written a beautiful eulogy for Ian on the Switchee blog.

Printed in Great Britain
by Amazon